party

dips!

party
dips!

50 zippy, zesty, spicy, savory, tasty, tempting dips

sally sampson

THE HARVARD COMMON PRESS
BOSTON, MASSACHUSETTS

The Harvard Common Press
535 Albany Street
Boston, Massachusetts 02118
www.harvardcommonpress.com

Printed in China

Library of Congress Cataloging-in-Publication Data
Sampson, Sally
    Party dips! : 50 zippy, zesty, spicy, savory, tasty, tempting dips / Sally Sampson.
        p. cm.
    Includes index.
    ISBN 1-55832-278-7 (hc : alk. paper)
1. Dips (Appetizers) I. Title
    TX740.S287 2004
    641.8'12-dc22
                                                        2004003193

Book and jacket design by Elizabeth Van Itallie
Photography by Eric Roth Photography
Food preparation and styling by David Kasabian
Props included on pages 41 and 73 were generously provided by Le Creuset of America, Inc.

Special bulk-order discounts are available on this and other Harvard Common Press book.
Companies and organizations may purchase books for premiums or resale, or may arrange a
custom edition, by contacting the Marketing Director at the address above.

10 9 8 7 6 5 4 3 2 1

For my mother, Sue Nirenberg,

who introduced me to the wonder of dips

For my husband, Mark, who dipped me,

and for my little dippers, Ben and Lauren

table of
contents

Introduction

As someone who loves to focus my creativity, energy, and time (all of which are limited) on the main course and dessert, I have never really enjoyed making hors d'oeuvres or typical cocktail fare. My goal is to spend a small amount of time on big, delicious foods rather than hours and hours painstakingly preparing canapés, stuffing mushrooms, or skewering shrimp, the end result of which does not, to me, justify the time and precision. Or as my 11-year-old daughter, Lauren, says, "At least if you spend a lot of time making dinner, it will satisfy and fill you up, but little hors d'oeuvres, while they are tasty and look nice, are hard to make and don't satisfy."

And yet there is always that special time, just before dinner, when guests are arriving slowly and either just kicking back or getting to know each other, and they both need and deserve something delicious to eat.

Additionally, my husband, Mark, loves to have "pick-up" food around so that if dinner is late or he comes home starving, he can eat something to bridge the gap. And my children, Lauren and nine-year-old Ben, are always hungry at all hours of the day and, luckily for me, don't go for the usual junk most kids snack on. My solution for all such occasions? Special cheeses, marinated olives, and dips: all I have to do is unwrap the cheeses, sprinkle some spices and oil on some olives, pull out my food processor and whip up a dip, cut up some vegetables, and, *voilà*, I am, as my mother used to say, the hostess with the mostest.

With a fridge packed with a reasonable arsenal of ingredients and a well-stocked pantry, preparing dips is speedy, trouble free, relatively inexpensive, and always a sensation. Moreover, with almost everyone I know on Atkins, the Zone, South Beach, or Weight Watchers, I have found that there is always a dip to satisfy not only every meal and palate but also every diet and special craving.

And truthfully, I have always had a special affection for dips. When my husband and I became engaged to be married, we decided to tell his parents in person. Without telling them the news, we called, suggesting we come for dinner. At past visits, his parents, George and Pattie, were always warm and welcoming to me; however, I was probably nothing like what they had imagined for their firstborn. Older by seven years, Jewish while he was Catholic, New York City born and raised to his more sheltered Hingham, Massachusetts, upbringing, I was independent in ways they found alien.

The dreaded and exciting moment came: we were sitting on tall kitchen stools surrounding a countertop overflowing with appetizers: crudités, dips, hot things, cold things. Mark said, "Mom, Dad: Sally and I got engaged." Dead silence. And then George, not missing a beat, grabbed a platter of artfully cut vegetables, looked up, and said, "Dip?"

Well, yes, the rest is history, but Mark and I can't even look at a dip without a certain amount of amusement. For the past 12 years, we have been on the lookout for great dips, if only to be able to offer each other some and say, "Dip?"

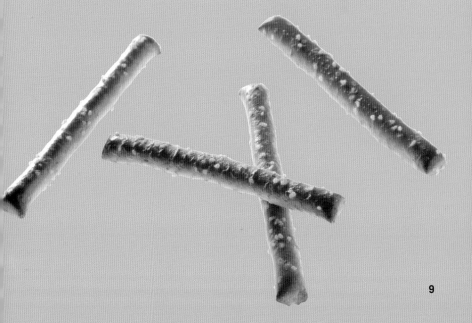

party dip

basics

1

There's a reason dips are part of almost everyone's party repertoire—they're easy to prepare, they can be made ahead or put together at the last minute, and they're always satisfying. This chapter covers the basics—ingredients to have on hand for emergency dip making, dippers, dip presentation, and some party dip building block recipes.

party dip
planning

The yields for all the recipes in this book are given in cups. When deciding how much dip or how many dips to make for a get-together, plan on a ¼-cup serving per person. Also, all the recipes in this book can be doubled, tripled, or quadrupled to accommodate your particular party needs.

The Party Dip Pantry

The great thing about dips is that if you have an assortment of items in your pantry and refrigerator, like those listed below, it's easy to throw something delicious together at a moment's notice. Of course, a garden full of fresh herbs also helps, but barring that, a good selection of dried herbs and spices is essential.

- Canned artichoke hearts
- Canned beans: cannellini (white beans), black, garbanzo (chickpeas), dark red kidney
- Canned tuna in water
- Oil-packed anchovies
- Capers in brine or salt
- Fresh garlic
- Olives
- Olive oil
- Mango chutney
- Cream cheese
- Sour cream
- Plain yogurt
- Mayonnaise

Impeccable Dippers

Gone are the days when you could just put out one bowl of chips and another of dip made with onion soup mix (not that I have anything against onion dip; see Lauren's Caramelized Onion Dip, page 33). Not only do dips taste better with a range of fresh dippers, it's also a healthier and more interesting way to eat them. And maybe this will cause you to eat more vegetables (always a good thing).

PREPPING VEGGIES FOR THE CRUDITÉS TRAY

• **Asparagus:** Trim off the bottom third and remove the outer skin with a vegetable peeler.

• **Bell peppers:** Cut off the top and bottom, make a slit along the side, then lay the pepper out flat. Remove the seeds and membranes, then cut into ½-inch-wide strips.

• **Broccoli:** Separate the florets from the stems. Peel the stems with a vegetable peeler.

• **Carrots:** Use baby carrots, or peel regular-size carrots and cut into thin sticks.

• **Cauliflower:** Separate the florets from the stems, discarding the stems.

• **Celery:** Use the inner ribs or remove the outer skin of the large stalks with a vegetable peeler. Cut into the size lengths you prefer, then cut each one again lengthwise into sticks.

• **Cherry tomatoes:** Leave whole and spear with toothpicks.

• **Cucumbers:** Peel, if not using European cucumbers, and either thinly slice or cut into quarters lengthwise, seed if necessary, and cut into spears.

• **Endive:** Remove the root and separate the leaves.

• **Fennel:** Trim and discard the feathery tops and stalks. Split the bulb in half lengthwise and remove the core. Cut into ½-inch-thick strips.

• **Green beans:** Trim the ends.

- **Jicama:** Peel and slice into rounds, then cut those into ½-inch-wide strips.
- **Radishes:** Trim the root ends and slice or halve.
- **Snow or sugar snap peas:** Remove the fibrous strings.

To Blanch or Not to Blanch

The truth is, I like most vegetables raw, but blanching is recommended for some vegetables, to make them both more tender to the tooth and brighter to the eye. Not all vegetables need to be blanched, especially if you are in a rush, but many benefit from a quick bath. To do it, have ready a bowl of ice water and a plate of several layers of clean dish towels or paper towels. Bring a large pot of water to a boil over high heat and add 1 to 2 tablespoons kosher salt. Add the vegetables, *one type at a time*, and leave in until crisp-tender: asparagus will take 30 seconds, broccoli and cauliflower florets, fennel bulb slices, and green beans 1 minute.

Immediately transfer to the ice water until completely cooled, 1 to 2 minutes, then place on the paper towels to dry.

Each time you blanch another vegetable, let the water return to a boil. Be sure to add broccoli and cauliflower last, as they will leave their flavor behind in the water.

BREAD, CHIPS, AND CRACKERS

The range of crackers, breads, and chips available is virtually endless. I seem to find new ones with each visit to the grocery store. While I have made specific dipper recommendations for each recipe, what you end up choosing should really be a matter of your own taste. I suggest you keep experimenting until you find the perfect fit. Below is a short list of the basics.

- Black bread
- Cocktail rye squares
- French bread, fresh or toasted
- Pita bread, fresh or toasted
- Bagel chips
- Corn chips
- Pita chips
- Potato chips
- Tortilla chips
- Crackers

Presenting . . .

Stuffing dips into loaves of bread (which get soggy) and hollowed-out cabbages (which get smelly) was very big in the 1970s and '80s, but frankly I'd rather put my time, energy, and money into finding great bowls and platters. Scour stores like Crate & Barrel and Williams-Sonoma (which sells bowls that look like hollowed-out cabbages), and certainly check out garage and tag sales. And be liberal with fresh herb garnishes!

Party Dip Building Blocks

Following are a few recipes that will give your dips and spreads that extra something special.

Yogurt Cheese

I use only lowfat or full-fat yogurt to make this component: when you make yogurt cheese with nonfat yogurt, the result is chalky. However, if you are used to the flavor of nonfat, it might be a viable alternative for you. Yogurt cheese is a terrific substitute for both sour cream and cream cheese in all the recipes in this book. I suggest you try it with other recipes, too.

One 32-ounce container lowfat or full-fat plain yogurt

1. Line a colander with muslin or cheesecloth. Place the colander over a large mixing bowl. Place the yogurt in the colander, cover with plastic wrap, and refrigerate at least 4 hours and up to overnight.
2. Discard the liquid that has drained into the bowl. Transfer the yogurt cheese to a small mixing bowl and use as directed in recipes, or cover and refrigerate for up to 4 days.

MAKES ABOUT 2 CUPS

Roasted Garlic

When I want a strong garlic flavor but not too much garlic pungency, I substitute roasted garlic for fresh. You can use this in any recipe calling for fresh garlic for a different taste twist.

1 head garlic
⅛ teaspoon kosher salt
1 tablespoon olive oil

1. Preheat the oven to 450°F.
2. Remove as much of the peel from the garlic as possible, being careful to keep the head intact. Place the garlic on a large piece of aluminum foil, sprinkle with the salt, drizzle with the oil, and wrap the foil around it.
3. Roast until the garlic is soft and tender, about 45 minutes. When cool enough to handle, squeeze the garlic from the peels and, if using it as a puree, mash with a fork. Cover and refrigerate for up to 1 week.

MAKES ABOUT 2½ TABLESPOONS, DEPENDING ON SIZE OF GARLIC HEAD

Roasted Bell Peppers

Roasted bell peppers can be substituted for fresh bell peppers in any recipe. They're great to have around anyway, as a tasty addition to sandwiches and omelets. You can't even compare them to those you can buy in jars—it's like the difference between fresh and frozen orange juice.

Bell peppers, any color

1. Preheat the broiler or oven to 400°F.
2. Place the peppers directly under the broiler or in the oven and cook until blackened on all sides.
3. Place the peppers in a heavy plastic or paper bag, close, and let sweat for about 10 minutes. Remove from the bag, remove the burned skin, then stem and seed the peppers. Slice as desired and use immediately, or store in the refrigerator for up to 3 weeks.

Toasting Nuts

Preheat the oven to 350°F. Spread the nuts in a single layer on a baking sheet. Bake until lightly browned, 10 to 12 minutes for pistachios, pine nuts, pecans, peanuts, and walnuts and 12 to 15 minutes for almonds, hazelnuts, and macadamia nuts. Set aside to cool. Cover and freeze for up to 1 month.

smooth
dips

2

- Herby Cream Cheese Dip
- Chickpea and Caramelized Onion Dip
- Ranch Dip
- Peppery Watercress Spread
- Creamy Almond-Basil Pesto Dip
- Roasted Red Pepper Aioli
- Ben's Chipotle Dip
- Caesar Aioli
- Creamy Avocado Dip with Mint and Basil
- Stan Frankenthaler's Green Goddess Dip
- Lauren's Caramelized Onion Dip
- Roasted Red Pepper Dip with Pomegranate Molasses
- Joey Steinberg's Cookie Dip
- Creamy Sesame Dip
- Classic Hummus
- Bagna Cauda
- Red Bean and Chipotle Chile Dip
- Garlicky Fava Bean Dip with Basil
- Smoked Trout Pâté with Horseradish Cream
- Salmon, Caviar, and Chive Dip
- Curried Tuna Dip
- Anchovy, Tuna, and White Bean Dip
- Cranberry Chutney Cream Cheese Dip

Herby Cream Cheese Dip

After I graduated from college, I worked at Essential Ingredients, a specialty market in Boulder, Colorado. Composed of two connected store fronts, one side carrying ingredients and the other prepared foods, it was way, way ahead of its time. This creamy, savory herb cheese was on the menu every day, and I ate it as a dip, a filling for omelets, a spread on sandwiches (smoked ham and honey mustard is a particularly good combo), and a topping for hamburgers. I have barely changed the recipe in all these years.

Two 8-ounce packages cream cheese, at room temperature, or 2 cups Yogurt Cheese (page 16)
$\frac{1}{4}$ to $\frac{1}{2}$ cup buttermilk, as needed
2 garlic cloves, minced
3 tablespoons finely chopped fresh Italian parsley leaves, plus more for garnish
1 tablespoon finely chopped fresh basil leaves
1 teaspoon finely chopped fresh oregano leaves
$\frac{1}{2}$ teaspoon dried thyme
$\frac{1}{2}$ teaspoon freshly ground black pepper
Kosher salt to taste

1. Place the cream cheese in a medium-size mixing bowl and mash with a fork. Gradually add the buttermilk until it achieves the consistency of cake icing, mashing until well incorporated. Add the remaining ingredients and mix until well combined.

2. Transfer to a small serving bowl and serve immediately, garnished with parsley, or cover and refrigerate for up to 1 week.

MAKES 2 $\frac{1}{2}$ TO 3 CUPS

DIVINE DIPPERS BAGEL OR PITA CHIPS OR THE CRUDITÉS OF YOUR CHOICE

Chickpea and Caramelized Onion Dip

Coarser and subtler than Classic Hummus (page 38), this rendition has a great herby taste that also works well as a sandwich spread (with tomatoes) or on burgers.

3 tablespoons olive oil
1 medium-size red onion, chopped
2 garlic cloves, minced
1½ teaspoons ground cumin
1 teaspoon dried Greek oregano
One 15.5-ounce can chickpeas, drained and rinsed
2 tablespoons water
2 tablespoons fresh lemon juice
¼ teaspoon kosher salt
¼ teaspoon cayenne pepper (optional)
Lemon slices for garnish

1. Place a large nonstick skillet over very low heat and add 1 tablespoon of the oil. When it is hot, add the onion, garlic, cumin, and oregano and cook, stirring a few times, until the onion is lightly browned, about 20 minutes. If it dries out at all, add water, 1 tablespoon at a time. Set aside to cool.

2. Transfer the cooled onion mixture to a food processor, add the chickpeas, and process until smooth. Add the 2 tablespoons water, the remaining 2 tablespoons oil, lemon juice, salt, and cayenne, if desired, and process until smooth.

3. Transfer to a serving bowl and serve immediately, garnished with the lemon slices, or cover and refrigerate for up to 2 days.

MAKES ABOUT 2 CUPS

DIVINE DIPPERS PITA CHIPS OR WARMED PITA TRIANGLES

Ranch Dip

I have to admit that I have only had ranch dressing from a bottle, and even that only a few times. But my daughter, Lauren, loves it, and I thought it would be great to have a homemade version. If you want to use it as a salad dressing, simply add more buttermilk until it reaches the desired consistency.

⅓ cup sour cream or Yogurt Cheese (page 16)
½ cup mayonnaise
¼ cup buttermilk
¼ cup finely diced or grated red onion
2 tablespoons finely chopped celery leaves
2 tablespoons finely chopped fresh chives
1 garlic clove, finely chopped
1 teaspoon fresh lemon juice
1 teaspoon finely grated lemon zest
Kosher salt and freshly ground black pepper to taste

1. Place all the ingredients in a medium-size mixing bowl and stir until well combined.
2. Transfer to a serving bowl, cover, and refrigerate at least 1 hour before serving and up to 8 hours.

MAKES 1½ CUPS

 DIVINE DIPPERS STEAMED TINY NEW POTATOES STILL IN THEIR JACKETS

Peppery Watercress Spread

The slightly stinging bite of the watercress is the perfect complement to
the velvety rich cream cheese. Though I mostly serve this as a dip, it's a
terrific and effortless addition to an omelet.

Watercress is a cousin to broccoli, kale, and mustard greens, all
members of the cruciferous vegetable family. Ancient Greeks thought it
would cure a deranged mind. It turns out that Popeye would have been
better off eating watercress, since it contains about seven times more
iron than spinach (and more calcium than milk!).

Sprigs from 1 bunch watercress (about 2 cups)
One 8-ounce package cream cheese, at room temperature, or 1 cup Yogurt
   Cheese (page 16)
$\frac{1}{2}$ to 1 teaspoon kosher salt, to your taste
$\frac{1}{4}$ teaspoon freshly ground black pepper

1. Place the watercress, reserving 2 sprigs for garnish, in a food
processor and process until chopped. Add the remaining ingredients
and process until well combined.

2. Serve immediately, garnished with the reserved watercress sprigs,
or cover and refrigerate for up to 1 week.

Variation: Substitute goat cheese for the cream cheese.

MAKES ABOUT 1 $\frac{1}{2}$ CUPS

DIVINE DIPPERS TORTILLA OR PITA CHIPS OR THE CRUDITÉS OF YOUR CHOICE

Creamy Almond-Basil Pesto Dip

This pesto is made with almonds instead of pine nuts and since it's mixed with lots of creamy things, don't think of it as a substitute for classic pesto. It's great on burgers and grilled chicken, too.

¼ cup whole almonds, toasted (page 17)
2 garlic cloves, peeled
1½ cups fresh basil leaves, plus more for garnish
1 tablespoon olive oil
¼ cup freshly grated Parmesan cheese
4 ounces cream cheese (half an 8-ounce package), at room temperature, or ½ cup Yogurt Cheese (page 16)
½ cup sour cream, full-fat plain yogurt, or Yogurt Cheese (page 16)
½ teaspoon kosher salt

1. Place the almonds and garlic in a food processor and pulse until well chopped. Add the basil and pulse again until chopped. While the machine is running, gradually add the oil through the feed tube, and process until smooth. Add the remaining ingredients and process until thick.

2. Transfer to a serving bowl, cover, and refrigerate for at least 1 hour and up to 3 days. Serve garnished with basil leaves.

MAKES ABOUT 2 CUPS

 DIVINE DIPPERS BABY CARROTS OR CARROT STICKS, CELERY STICKS, ENDIVE, JICAMA STICKS OR SLICES, OR STEAMED TINY NEW POTATOES

Roasted Red Pepper Aioli

Silky and yet slightly chunky, this bright pink aioli is great for vegetable dipping as well as for slathering on roast beef sandwiches and drizzling over grilled steak. When you are preparing it, be sure to add the oils very slowly so that the mixture emulsifies properly. (If you don't, it will be too thin, but then you can simply use it as a salad dressing.)

2 large red bell peppers, roasted, peeled, and seeded (page 17), and cut into large chunks
1 garlic clove, peeled
2 tablespoons fresh lemon juice
2 very fresh large egg yolks (see Note on page 29)
1 teaspoon water
$1/2$ cup canola oil
$1/2$ cup olive oil
$1/2$ teaspoon kosher salt
$1/4$ to $1/2$ teaspoon cayenne pepper or chipotle chile powder, to your taste
Freshly ground black pepper to taste
Chopped fresh Italian parsley for garnish (optional)

1. Place the red peppers and garlic in a food processor and pulse until well chopped but not minced. Add the lemon juice and egg yolks and process until well incorporated. While the machine is running, add the water, then gradually add the oils, 1 tablespoon at a time, through the feed tube and process until smooth. Add the salt and cayenne, season with black pepper, and process until thick.

2. Transfer to a serving bowl, cover, and refrigerate for at least 1 hour and up to 8 hours. Serve chilled, garnished with parsley, if desired.

MAKES ABOUT $2 1/2$ CUPS

DIVINE DIPPERS BOILED TINY NEW POTATOES, BLANCHED ASPARAGUS OR BROCCOLI FLORETS, ENDIVE SPEARS, RADISHES, PITA CHIPS, OR FRENCH BREAD TOASTS

Ben's Chipotle Dip

When I first made this dip, my nine-year-old son, Ben, declared: "Mom, this is the best dip of yours I have ever had." He is no ordinary mac and cheese/pizza/cheeseburger kind of kid. Ben loves spicy food and while he doesn't really like creamy food, this combination hit the spot. Chipotles are smoked jalapeño peppers and add both heat and deep smoky flavor to dishes. They are available at any supermarket with a good ethnic section or at specialty stores.

One 8-ounce package cream cheese or goat cheese, at room temperature
²/₃ cup sour cream
2 to 3 teaspoons fresh lime juice, to your taste
3 canned chipotle chiles in adobo sauce, minced (about 3 tablespoons)
2 tablespoons minced scallions (green part only), plus more for garnish
2 to 3 tablespoons minced fresh cilantro or basil leaves, to your taste
Finely grated zest of 1 well-washed lime

1. Place the cream cheese, sour cream, and lime juice in a food processor and process until creamy. Stir in the remaining ingredients by hand.

2. Transfer to a serving bowl and serve immediately, garnished with scallions, or cover and refrigerate for up to 1 week.

MAKES ABOUT 2 CUPS

DIVINE DIPPERS BLANCHED ASPARAGUS, CELERY STICKS, OR ENDIVE SPEARS, OR PITA, BAGEL, OR POTATO CHIPS

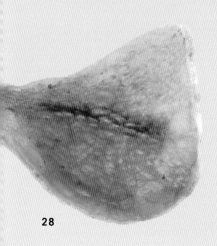

Caesar Aioli

What more could you want than the great taste of Caesar dressing in a dip? Don't be tempted to leave out the anchovies—they are rich in omega-3 oils, calcium, and iron. If you find your anchovies are too salty, soak them in cold water for half an hour, then drain.

1 garlic clove, peeled
2 tablespoons fresh lemon juice
2 very fresh large egg yolks
1 cup olive oil
1 teaspoon water
2 tablespoons Dijon mustard
2 oil-packed anchovy fillets
$\frac{1}{2}$ cup freshly grated Parmesan cheese
$\frac{1}{2}$ teaspoon kosher salt
Freshly ground black pepper to taste
Strips of lemon zest for garnish

1. Place the garlic in a food processor and pulse until well chopped but not minced. Add the lemon juice and egg yolks and process until well incorporated. While the machine is running, gradually add the oil, 1 tablespoon at a time, through the feed tube, and process until smooth. Add the remaining ingredients, except the lemon zest, and process until thick.

2. Transfer to a serving bowl. Cover and refrigerate at least 1 hour or up to 8 hours. Serve garnished with the lemon zest.

Note: Because this recipe contains raw eggs, it's a good idea when serving this to keep it chilled: place it in a bowl, then place that bowl in a larger bowl filled with ice.

MAKES ABOUT 1 $\frac{1}{2}$ CUPS

 DIVINE DIPPERS STEAMED TINY NEW POTATOES, ASPARAGUS, BROCCOLI FLORETS, ENDIVE SPEARS, RADISHES, PITA CHIPS, OR FRENCH BREAD TOASTS

Creamy Avocado Dip with Mint and Basil

Although I am a huge, huge fan of guacamole, I still wanted an avocado dip that was lighter and, well, just different. This one is creamy and mild, unless, of course, you choose to add some cayenne, chipotle, or hot sauce. This also happens to be sensational drizzled on grilled steak, stuffed into omelets, or substituted for mayonnaise in cheese and tomato sandwiches.

4 very ripe avocados, pitted, peeled, and mashed
1 heaping tablespoon finely chopped fresh mint leaves
2 tablespoons finely chopped fresh basil leaves, plus more for garnish
Juice and finely grated zest of 2 well-washed limes
2 tablespoons heavy cream
$\frac{1}{2}$ to 1 teaspoon kosher salt, to your taste
$\frac{1}{4}$ teaspoon cayenne pepper or chipotle chile powder, to your taste (optional)
$\frac{1}{2}$ to 1 teaspoon Tabasco sauce, to your taste (optional)

1. Place everything in a medium-size mixing bowl and mash together well.
2. Transfer to a serving bowl and serve immediately, garnished with chopped basil, or cover and refrigerate for no more than 1 hour before serving, as the avocado will begin to discolor.

MAKES ABOUT 2 CUPS

 DIVINE DIPPERS ENDIVE SPEARS, RED BELL PEPPER STRIPS, OR TORTILLA CHIPS

Stan Frankenthaler's Green Goddess Dip

Created in honor of actor George Arliss, who was appearing in a play called *The Green Goddess*, written by William Archer, green goddess dressing was introduced during the 1920s by the chef at San Francisco's Palace Hotel (where Arliss was staying). Arliss was later nominated for an Academy Award for his performance in the film version but lost out to himself, for his role as Prime Minister Benjamin Disraeli.

Thick, creamy, herby, and decidedly old-fashioned, this dip was inspired by Boston chef Stan Frankenthaler's green goddess salad dressing. Also try it on grilled, broiled, or steamed fish.

1 garlic clove, sliced
2 to 3 oil-packed anchovy fillets, to your taste
1 tablespoon capers, drained
$\frac{1}{2}$ cup spinach leaves, washed well and patted dry
2 scallions (white and green parts)
$\frac{1}{4}$ cup fresh Italian parsley leaves, plus more for garnish
2 sprigs fresh tarragon
$\frac{1}{4}$ cup sour cream or Yogurt Cheese (page 16)
$\frac{1}{4}$ cup mayonnaise
$\frac{1}{4}$ teaspoon freshly ground black pepper (optional)

1. Place the garlic, anchovies, capers, spinach, scallions, parsley, and tarragon in a blender or food processor and process until smooth. Add the sour cream and blend again until smooth. Stir in the mayonnaise and pepper, if desired, and mix to combine.

2. Transfer to a serving bowl and serve immediately, garnished with parsley leaves, or cover and refrigerate for up to 1 week.

MAKES ABOUT 1 CUP

DIVINE DIPPERS THIS IS SPLENDID WITH SOMETHING SLIGHTLY BITTER LIKE ENDIVE, BUT ALMOST ANY VEGETABLE WORKS, ESPECIALLY LIGHTLY STEAMED ASPARAGUS SPEARS OR BABY ARTICHOKES.

Lauren's Caramelized Onion Dip

Everyone seems to like dip made from onion soup mix and since that isn't really my style, I decided to come up with a, shall we say, fresher version. Salty, creamy, sweet, and rich, this is my daughter Lauren's idea of heaven.

1 tablespoon olive oil
1 tablespoon unsalted butter
1 large or 2 small red onions, thinly sliced and chopped
1 teaspoon chopped fresh rosemary leaves
$\frac{1}{2}$ cup sour cream or Yogurt Cheese (page 16)
$\frac{1}{2}$ cup mayonnaise
$\frac{1}{4}$ teaspoon kosher salt
$\frac{1}{4}$ teaspoon freshly ground black pepper (if Lauren isn't eating it)
1 scallion (green part only), chopped, for garnish

1. Place a medium-size skillet over low heat and, when it is hot, add the oil and butter. When the butter melts, add the onions and rosemary and cook, stirring occasionally, until the onions are deeply browned and caramelized, 35 to 40 minutes. Transfer to a small mixing bowl and let cool.

2. Add the sour cream, mayonnaise, salt, and pepper, and mix to combine.

3. Transfer to a small serving bowl. Serve immediately, garnished with the scallion, or cover and refrigerate for up to 2 days.

MAKES 1 TO 1$\frac{1}{4}$ CUPS

DIVINE DIPPERS LAUREN LIKES THIS BEST WITH PITA CHIPS BUT ALSO ENJOYS IT WITH CRUDITÉS AND TORTILLA CHIPS. I LIKE IT WITH TRIANGLES OF THINLY SLICED DARK PUMPERNICKEL BREAD.

Roasted Red Pepper Dip with Pomegranate Molasses

I first had this exotic and unusual dip at a local restaurant called the Blue Room when it was owned and run by chef Chris Schlesinger. When I couldn't figure out the ingredients, Chris generously shared the recipe with me.

The most unusual ingredient is the pomegranate molasses, considered by some to be the balsamic vinegar of the future. A deep red, tart, almost astringent, thick syrup, the name molasses is somewhat of a misnomer, as its sweetness comes from the concentration of the fruit rather than from sugar. You can find pomegranate molasses in any supermarket with a large ethnic section or in Armenian or Arab specialty markets.

1 tablespoon olive oil
1 Spanish onion, chopped
2 garlic cloves, minced
1 tablespoon light brown sugar
1 tablespoon ground cumin
3 red bell peppers, roasted, peeled, and seeded (page 17)
1 cup walnuts, toasted (page 17)
Juice of 1 lime
2 tablespoons pomegranate molasses
3 tablespoons chopped fresh Italian parsley leaves, plus more for garnish

1. Place a large skillet over medium-high heat and, when it is hot, add the oil. Add the onion, garlic, brown sugar, and cumin and cook, stirring, until the onion is slightly caramelized, about 10 minutes. Transfer to a food processor, add the remaining ingredients, and process until smooth.

2. Transfer to a serving bowl, cover, and refrigerate for at least 1 hour and up to 2 days to let the flavors develop. Serve garnished with chopped parsley.

MAKES ABOUT 2 CUPS

DIVINE DIPPERS WARMED PITA TRIANGLES

Joey Steinberg's Cookie Dip

One Valentine's Day, I called my friend Nancy to check out the amount of parsley in her friend Joan Goldberg's dip (page 59). She wasn't home, and when I asked her husband, Steve, for a dip idea, he suggested I ask his five-year-old son, Joey. Here is Joey's dip. I am sorry I don't have the ability to reproduce our conversation, replete with Joey's at once serious and exasperated tone.

2 tablespoons smooth peanut butter (Jif)
½ pint ice cream ("maybe vanilla or chocolate or both"), softened in the microwave till it's mushable
Small splash of milk ("I use whole milk," says Joey.)

"Put everything in a bowl and mush it all together," instructs Joey.
"What would you dip in it?" I ask.
"Cookies," he says, a bit irked, as if it's obvious. "Christmas cookies."
"What if it isn't Christmas?" I ask.
"Well, then," he says, "big, medium, and little hearts. Or stars, for nighttime. Paint them with a little frosting," he adds. "Pink for Lauren [my daughter] and blue for Ben [my son]."
"What about for you?" I ask.
"Yellow for me."
"And what about for Charlie [Joey's brother]?"
"Blue. Charlie likes blue too. Okay, bye." And he hangs up.
Serve immediately.

Creamy Sesame Dip

Though this combination of flavors is most often seen on Asian noodles, it translates wonderfully into a creamy, spicy dip. Don't leave out the tea—it adds an ineffable smokiness.

2 tablespoons sesame seeds for garnish
1 cup mayonnaise
$1/2$ cup tahini
$1/2$ cup brewed black tea, at room temperature
2 garlic cloves, minced
2 tablespoons rice vinegar
$1^{1}/_{2}$ tablespoons soy sauce
2 teaspoons Dijon mustard
1 teaspoon chili powder
$1/4$ to $1/2$ teaspoon cayenne pepper, to your taste
1 scallion (white and green parts), chopped, for garnish

1. Place the sesame seeds in a small skillet and toast over medium heat until lightly browned, about 3 minutes. Set aside to cool.

2. Place the mayonnaise, tahini, tea, garlic, vinegar, soy sauce, mustard, chili powder, and cayenne in a food processor and process until smooth.

3. Transfer to a serving bowl, cover, and refrigerate for at least 1 hour and up to 2 days to let the flavors develop. Garnish with the chopped scallion and sesame seeds.

MAKES $1^{3}/_{4}$ TO 2 CUPS

 DIVINE DIPPERS SNOW PEAS, RED AND GREEN BELL PEPPER STRIPS, OR BLANCHED ASPARAGUS

Classic Hummus

Hummus, the classic Middle Eastern dip of chickpeas, tahini (sesame paste), garlic, and lemon juice, is also known as *hummus bi tahini*. I like to vary the beans and the flavorings: variations include substituting chopped or pureed roasted bell or chile peppers or olives for the basil, or adding 1 tablespoon finely grated lemon, lime, or orange zest. White cannellini beans are an excellent stand-in for the chickpeas.

One 15.5-ounce can chickpeas, drained and rinsed
2 to 3 garlic cloves, to your taste, crushed, or 1 head garlic, roasted and
  squeezed out of the skin (page 16)
3 to 4 tablespoons tahini, to your taste
1 tablespoons extra-virgin olive oil
3 tablespoons fresh lemon juice
$\frac{1}{2}$ teaspoon ground cumin, or more to your taste (optional)
$\frac{1}{2}$ teaspoon kosher salt
$\frac{1}{2}$ to 1 cup chopped fresh basil or cilantro leaves, scallions (white and green
  parts), or chives or a combination (optional), to your taste
Freshly ground black pepper to taste
Lemon, lime, or orange slices for garnish
Paprika for garnish

1. Place the chickpeas and garlic in a food processor and process until smooth. Gradually add the tahini, olive oil, lemon juice, cumin, if desired, and salt and process until completely smooth. Add the basil, if desired, and process until fully incorporated. Season with pepper.

2. Transfer to a serving bowl and serve immediately, garnished with the lemon slices and paprika, or cover and refrigerate for up to 2 days.

MAKES ABOUT 1 $\frac{1}{2}$ CUPS

 DIVINE DIPPERS CELERY STICKS, BABY CARROTS OR CARROT STICKS, SNOW PEAS, BLANCHED CAULIFLOWER FLORETS, OR PITA OR BAGEL CHIPS

Bagna Cauda

Translated as "hot bath," this specialty of Piedmont, Italy, is often part of the Italian Christmas Eve buffet. Traditionally, slices of cardoon (an edible celery-like member of the artichoke family) are dipped into the sauce, then eaten with a slice of bread held underneath to catch the drippings. It must be served hot, so serve it in a dish that can be placed over a little warmer, or serve it from a small slow cooker.

1 cup extra virgin olive oil
4 garlic cloves, crushed, or 1 head garlic, roasted and squeezed out of the
   skin (page 16)
One 2-ounce can oil-packed anchovies, drained
3 tablespoons unsalted butter, at room temperature
Freshly ground black pepper to taste
1/4 cup heavy cream (optional)

1. Place the oil in a medium-size skillet over medium heat. When it is warm, add the garlic and anchovies and cook, stirring and mashing the anchovies constantly, until they disintegrate, about 3 minutes. Add the butter and stir until incorporated into the mixture. Season with pepper. Stir in the cream, if desired.

2. Transfer to a heatproof serving bowl or a small slow cooker and serve immediately.

MAKES 1¼ CUPS

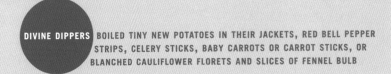

DIVINE DIPPERS BOILED TINY NEW POTATOES IN THEIR JACKETS, RED BELL PEPPER STRIPS, CELERY STICKS, BABY CARROTS OR CARROT STICKS, OR BLANCHED CAULIFLOWER FLORETS AND SLICES OF FENNEL BULB

Red Bean and Chipotle Chile Dip

I came up with this dip completely by mistake. My guests were on the way, and I had no time to spare and wasn't paying attention when, hoping to make hummus, I threw red beans instead of chickpeas into the food processor. When I realized my mistake, it was too late, so I made a few changes to the recipe and discovered I liked this one even better. You can try this recipe using any kind of bean.

Chipotle chile powder (smoked jalapeño) is available through the Penzeys catalog (414-574-0277 or www.penzeys.com). You can use it anywhere you might use cayenne pepper; it lends a wonderful smokiness.

One 15.5-ounce can dark red kidney beans, drained and rinsed
2 garlic cloves, peeled
$1/4$ cup orange juice
$1/2$ teaspoon ground cumin
$1/2$ teaspoon kosher salt
$1/4$ to $1/2$ teaspoon chipotle chile powder (if you can't find it, substitute cayenne pepper), to your taste
Juice of $1/2$ lime
2 tablespoons chopped fresh cilantro leaves

1. Place the beans, garlic, orange juice, cumin, salt, chipotle, lime juice, and 1 tablespoon of the cilantro in a food processor and process until smooth.

2. Transfer to a serving bowl and serve immediately, garnished with the remaining 1 tablespoon cilantro, or cover and refrigerate for up to 3 days.

MAKES $1^{1}/_{2}$ TO 2 CUPS

DIVINE DIPPERS PITA OR CORN CHIPS OR THE CRUDITÉS OF YOUR CHOICE

Garlicky Fava Bean Dip with Basil

Bright green and silky smooth, this recipe, yet another offshoot of hummus, was created by Lydia Shire and Susan Regis, two of Boston's most inspired and brilliant chefs.

1 cup shelled fresh fava beans
4 garlic cloves, chopped
$\frac{1}{4}$ cup olive oil
1 tablespoon fresh lemon juice
$\frac{1}{2}$ teaspoon kosher salt
$\frac{1}{2}$ teaspoon freshly ground black pepper
$\frac{1}{4}$ cup chopped fresh basil leaves
2 thin slices lemon for garnish

1. Place a large bowl of ice water on the counter. Bring a medium-size saucepan of water to a boil over high heat. Add the beans and cook until they turn bright green, about 2 minutes. Drain, then transfer to the ice bath for 1 minute and drain again. Peel the beans by pinching the end of each one; it will easily slip out.

2. Place the beans and garlic in a food processor and process until smooth. With the machine running, gradually add the olive oil, lemon juice, salt, and pepper through the feed tube and process until well incorporated. Stir in the basil by hand.

3. Transfer to a serving bowl and serve immediately, garnished with the lemon slices, or cover and refrigerate for up to 2 days.

MAKES ABOUT 1 CUP

DIVINE DIPPERS WARMED PITA TRIANGLES OR PITA CHIPS

Smoked Trout Pâté with Horseradish Cream

Smoky and creamy with a slight amount of graininess, this unusual dip will leave your guests wondering what's in it. If you can't find fresh horseradish, you can substitute bottled, but be sure it has no sugar in it.

¼ pound smoked trout
½ small red onion, chopped
Juice of 1 lemon, plus zest removed in thin strips for garnish
2 tablespoons peeled and grated fresh horseradish
3 tablespoons heavy cream
⅓ cup cream cheese or Yogurt Cheese (page 16)

1. Place the trout and onion in a food processor and pulse until chopped. Add the lemon juice, horseradish, heavy cream, and cream cheese and pulse until it comes together.
2. Transfer to a serving bowl, cover, and refrigerate at least 2 hours and up to 3 days to let the flavor develop. Serve garnished with the lemon strips.

MAKES ABOUT 1½ CUPS

DIVINE DIPPERS CRACKERS, TOAST POINTS, OR ENDIVE SPEARS

Salmon, Caviar, and Chive Dip

Very pale pink with green flecks, this delicate, beautiful dip lasts about two seconds in my house. It's great on any sandwich made with black bread, slathered on matzos and bagels, spooned into soups, or added to omelets.

4 ounces smoked salmon, shredded
2 scallions (green part only), chopped
$1/4$ cup chopped fresh chives, plus more for garnish
One 8-ounce package cream cheese, at room temperature, or 1 cup Yogurt
    Cheese (page 16)
$1/4$ cup milk
Juice and grated zest of 1 well-washed lime
Tabasco sauce to taste
2 tablespoons red salmon caviar for garnish

1. Place the salmon, scallions, and chives in a food processor and pulse until chopped. Add the cream cheese, milk, and lime juice and zest and pulse until it comes together. Season with the Tabasco.

2. Transfer to a serving bowl and serve immediately, garnished with the caviar and chopped chives, or cover and refrigerate for up to 1 week.

MAKES ABOUT 2 CUPS

 **DIVINE DIPPERS** CELERY STICKS, BABY CARROTS OR CARROT STICKS, ENDIVE SPEARS, OR PITA CHIPS

Curried Tuna Dip

This is a more delicate version of the traditional curried tuna, hefty enough to fill a tea sandwich but light enough for dipping.

One 6-ounce can white tuna packed in spring water, drained
2 tablespoons mayonnaise or olive oil
1 tablespoon orange juice
$\frac{1}{4}$ cup cooked white beans
$\frac{1}{2}$ teaspoon kosher salt
$1\frac{1}{2}$ teaspoons curry powder
2 tablespoons chopped fresh Italian parsley, cilantro, or basil leaves
2 orange slices for garnish

1. Place the tuna, mayonnaise, orange juice, beans, salt, and curry powder in a food processor and process until smooth. Add the parsley and stir by hand to combine.

2. Transfer to a serving bowl and serve immediately, garnished with the orange slices, or cover and refrigerate for up to 4 days.

MAKES ABOUT $1\frac{1}{2}$ CUPS

DIVINE DIPPERS BAGEL, PITA, OR CORN CHIPS OR THE CRUDITÉS OF YOUR CHOICE

Anchovy, Tuna, and White Bean Dip

This is a variation on a classic Italian salad.

1 cup cooked white beans
One 6-ounce can white tuna packed in spring water, drained
1 small anchovy fillet, rinsed
1 garlic clove, peeled
Juice of $\frac{1}{2}$ lemon
1 tablespoon capers, drained
$\frac{1}{2}$ teaspoon freshly ground black pepper
1 tablespoon chopped fresh Italian parsley leaves
1 tablespoon chopped fresh basil leaves
2 thin slices lemon for garnish

1. Place the beans, tuna, anchovy, garlic, lemon juice, capers, and pepper in a food processor and process until smooth. Add the parsley and basil and stir by hand to combine.

2. Transfer to a serving bowl and serve immediately, garnished with the lemon slices, or cover and refrigerate for up to 4 days.

MAKES ABOUT 1 $\frac{1}{2}$ CUPS

 DIVINE DIPPERS ENDIVE SPEARS, CROSTINI, OR FRENCH BREAD TOASTS

Cranberry Chutney Cream Cheese Dip

Creamy, rich, sweet, and spicy, this is a great dip for the customary lineup of vegetable dippers, as well as for fruit. I have included here the greatest-ever recipe for cranberry chutney, created by my longtime friend and editor Sydny Miner.

SYDNY MINER'S CRANBERRY CHUTNEY (MAKES 2 CUPS)
One 12-ounce bag fresh cranberries (3 cups), picked over for stems
$\frac{1}{4}$ cup orange juice
1 to 2 fresh jalapeño or canned chipotle chiles in adobo sauce, minced
$\frac{1}{2}$ cup firmly packed light brown sugar
$\frac{1}{2}$ teaspoon kosher salt
Grated zest of 1 well-washed lime
Grated zest of 1 well-washed orange
$\frac{3}{4}$ cup pecans or walnuts, toasted (page 17) and coarsely chopped

DIP
One 8-ounce package cream cheese, at room temperature, or 1 cup Yogurt
  Cheese (page 16)
$\frac{1}{2}$ cup cranberry chutney
1 teaspoon curry powder
1 scallion (white and green parts), finely chopped, for garnish

1. To make the chutney, place the cranberries, orange juice, chiles, and brown sugar in a medium-size nonreactive saucepan and cook over medium-high heat until the cranberries are soft and have absorbed all the liquid, about 10 minutes. Set aside to cool, then stir in the salt, zests, and nuts. Use immediately, or cover and refrigerate for up to 2 weeks.

2. To make the dip, place the cream cheese in a small mixing bowl and mash with a fork. Gradually add the chutney and curry powder and mash until well incorporated.

3. Transfer to a serving bowl and serve immediately, garnished with the scallion, or cover and refrigerate for up to 3 days. If refrigerated, let come to room temperature before serving, if desired.

MAKES 1 TO 1$\frac{1}{4}$ CUPS

DIVINE DIPPERS CRUDITÉS, ESPECIALLY CELERY STICKS, ENDIVE SPEARS, OR BLANCHED SLICES OF FENNEL BULB, AS WELL AS STRAWBERRIES OR APPLE SLICES

chunky dips

- Sun-Dried Tomato Tapenade
- Hot and Steamy Artichoke Dip
- New Orleans–Style Muffuletta Dip
- Artichoke and Feta Dip
- Artichoke and Prosciutto Dip
- Joan Goldberg's Light! Fresh! Delicious! Dip
- Basil Tapenade Dip
- Judith Shaw's Dip for Watch-Your-Weight Freaks
- Toni Oberholzer's Tsatziki
- Tropical Fruit Salsa
- Baba Ghanoush with Fresh Cilantro and Mint
- Lauren's Famous Guacamole
- Nancy Olin's Black Bean and Corn Salsa
- Mark's Classic Clam Dip
- David Tobias's Papa Harold's Chopped Chicken Liver Pâté
- Andy Husbands's Hot Crabmeat Dip

Sun-Dried Tomato Tapenade

This is a very rich dip that's also great on grilled swordfish, steak, and pork. If you find it too chunky, simply add a bit of mayonnaise.

1 cup loosely packed sun-dried tomatoes
$\frac{1}{2}$ cup boiling water
2 garlic cloves, chopped
$\frac{1}{4}$ cup packed fresh basil leaves
$\frac{1}{4}$ cup packed fresh Italian parsley leaves
2 tablespoons capers, drained
4 oil-packed anchovy fillets
1 tablespoon olive oil

1. Place the tomatoes and water in a medium-size heatproof bowl and let soften for 30 minutes.

2. Transfer the tomatoes and soaking water to a food processor and pulse until well chopped. Return the mixture to the bowl, add the remaining ingredients, and mix well.

3. Transfer to a serving bowl and serve immediately, or cover and refrigerate for up to 4 days.

MAKES ABOUT 1 $\frac{1}{2}$ CUPS

DIVINE DIPPERS WARMED PITA TRIANGLES OR CRACKERS

Hot and Steamy Artichoke Dip

My daughter, Lauren, describes this dish as looking odd but tasting great. She was sure a hot dip would be weird but demolished most of it herself.

One 6-ounce jar marinated artichoke hearts, drained and chopped
$1/4$ cup mayonnaise
$1/4$ cup sour cream
$1/3$ cup freshly grated Parmesan cheese
2 tablespoons finely minced red onion

1. Preheat the oven to 325°F.
2. Place all the ingredients in a medium-size mixing bowl and mix well. Transfer to a small casserole and bake until bubbling hot, about 15 minutes. Serve immediately from the casserole.

MAKES ABOUT 1 $1/2$ CUPS

 DIVINE DIPPERS THIS IS BEST WITH THICK TORTILLA CHIPS AND PITA CHIPS; IT REALLY DOESN'T PAIR WELL WITH CRUDITÉS OR THINNER CHIPS.

New Orleans–Style Muffuletta Dip

A muffuletta is a round hero-like sandwich that originated at the Central Grocery in New Orleans in the early 1900s. Layers of provolone cheese, Genoa salami, and ham are topped with an "olive salad," which is what distinguishes it from all other sandwiches. This chunky, salty, almost spicy dip does credit to its inspiration.

$\frac{1}{2}$ cup pitted Spanish green olives, drained
$\frac{1}{2}$ cup pitted brine-cured black olives (such as Kalamata), drained
$\frac{1}{4}$ cup coarsely chopped red onion
1 garlic clove, peeled
2 to 4 tablespoons chopped fresh basil or parsley leaves, to your taste
$\frac{1}{2}$ teaspoon dried Greek oregano
Juice of $\frac{1}{2}$ lemon (about 2 tablespoons)
1 teaspoon Dijon mustard
$\frac{1}{4}$ teaspoon Tabasco sauce, or more to taste
$\frac{1}{4}$ cup mayonnaise

1. Place the olives, onion, garlic, and basil in a food processor and pulse until chopped. Transfer to a small mixing bowl and stir in the remaining ingredients until well combined. Cover and refrigerate at least 1 hour and up to overnight to let the flavors develop.
2. Mix well, transfer to a serving bowl, and serve immediately.

MAKES ABOUT 1½ CUPS

DIVINE DIPPERS PITA CHIPS OR THIN SLICES OF TOAST

Artichoke and Feta Dip

This is the rare dip that contains as much vegetable as it does cheese. Chunky, salty, and light, it's one of my favorites.

Feta, the only cheese other than Parmesan that can always be found in my refrigerator, is a classic Greek white cheese that is both salty and tangy, a winning combination for me. Traditionally made from sheep or goat's milk, it is now mostly made with pasteurized cow's milk.

One 6-ounce jar marinated artichoke hearts, drained and coarsely chopped
$1/2$ cup sour cream or Yogurt Cheese (page 16)
2 garlic cloves, minced
1 oil-packed anchovy fillet, minced
$1/4$ cup crumbled feta cheese
$1/4$ teaspoon freshly ground black pepper
$1/4$ teaspoon kosher salt
1 teaspoon chopped fresh dill, plus more for garnish

1. Place all the ingredients in a small mixing bowl and gently combine.

2. Transfer to a serving bowl and serve immediately, garnished with chopped dill, or cover and refrigerate for up to 4 hours.

MAKES 1 TO $1 1/2$ CUPS

DIVINE DIPPERS CELERY STICKS, ENDIVE SPEARS, CRACKERS, OR FRENCH BREAD TOASTS

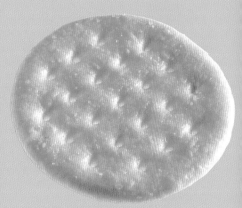

Artichoke and Prosciutto Dip

Inspired by a dip I tasted in an Italian restaurant, this artichoke lover's dip is salty, creamy, and tart. It is virtually impossible to leave even a drop of it in the bowl.

Prosciutto is an Italian ham, cured by dry-salting for one month followed by air-drying in cool curing sheds for half a year or longer. It is usually cut into tissue-thin slices that highlight its intense flavor and deep pink color. *Prosciutto di Parma,* imported from Italy, is widely regarded as the best, though it's not necessary to make this dip taste great; a domestic brand will work fine. Prosciutto can be kept refrigerated, well wrapped, for several weeks.

4 thin slices prosciutto, chopped
One 13.75-ounce can artichoke hearts (8 to 10), drained and rinsed
$\frac{1}{4}$ cup chopped fresh Italian parsley leaves or 2 tablespoons chopped fresh basil leaves, plus more for garnish
2 garlic cloves, sliced
Finely grated zest and juice of $\frac{1}{2}$ lemon
One 8-ounce container sour cream or 1 cup Yogurt Cheese (page 16)
$\frac{1}{4}$ cup mayonnaise

1. Place the prosciutto, artichoke hearts, parsley, and garlic in a food processor and pulse until chopped. Add the remaining ingredients and pulse until combined.

2. Transfer to a serving bowl and serve immediately, garnished with chopped parsley, or cover and refrigerate for up to 3 days.

MAKES 2 TO 2½ CUPS

 DIVINE DIPPERS FRENCH BREAD TOASTS OR PITA OR BAGEL CHIPS

Joan Goldberg's Light! Fresh! Delicious! Dip

My friend Nancy got this amusingly described summer dip recipe from her friend Joan Goldberg and, in fact, it lives up to its description, as she says.

One 16-ounce container sour cream or 2 cups Yogurt Cheese (page 16)
1 cup mayonnaise
2 medium-size cucumbers, peeled, seeded if desired, and finely chopped
2 cups packed fresh Italian parsley leaves, finely chopped
1 bunch scallions (white and green parts) or $\frac{1}{2}$ medium-size red onion, finely chopped
$\frac{1}{2}$ teaspoon freshly ground black pepper
$\frac{1}{4}$ teaspoon kosher salt

1. Place all the ingredients in a large mixing bowl and mix well.

2. Transfer to a serving bowl and serve immediately, or cover and refrigerate overnight.

MAKES 4 CUPS

DIVINE DIPPERS JOAN SAYS THAT FRITO-LAY'S RIDGED POTATO CHIPS ARE THE ONLY WAY TO GO.

Basil Tapenade Dip

This tapenade-like dip isn't the classic version but, rather, my interpretation of it. Not for anyone on a low-sodium diet, the combination of olives, anchovies, and capers makes for a wonderful, although incredibly salty, concoction. It's reminiscent of pesto in flavor, but saltier and brinier. Try it on grilled swordfish.

1 cup packed fresh basil leaves
$\frac{1}{2}$ cup pitted black Kalamata olives, drained
$\frac{1}{4}$ cup pitted green olives, drained
2 oil-packed anchovy fillets
2 garlic cloves, quartered
2 tablespoons capers, drained
1 tablespoon fresh lemon juice
$\frac{1}{4}$ cup olive oil
$\frac{1}{4}$ cup mayonnaise

1. Place the basil, olives, anchovies, garlic, and capers in a food processor and pulse until well chopped. While the machine is running, slowly add the lemon juice and olive oil through the feed tube and process until the mixture comes together. Stir in the mayonnaise by hand.

2. Transfer to a serving bowl and serve immediately, or cover and refrigerate for up to 2 days.

MAKES ABOUT 1$\frac{1}{4}$ CUPS

DIVINE DIPPERS UNSALTED CRACKERS OR ENDIVE SPEARS

Judith Shaw's Dip for Watch-Your-Weight Freaks

When I sent an e-mail to my friend Judith asking for dip recipes, she told me she didn't have any. Two days later, she sent this e-mail: "I guess in a way it's not true that I don't have a dip recipe. I will reluctantly call this a dip in deference to your need. But it's for rigid people (a.k.a. fat phobes) like me." Really more like a finely chopped salad, this dip is unusual and refreshing.

3 carrots, finely, finely chopped
3 celery stalks, finely, finely chopped
1 small red onion, finely, finely chopped
Juice of 1 lime
Kosher salt and freshly ground black pepper to taste

1. Place all the ingredients in a medium-size mixing bowl and combine well.
2. Transfer to a serving bowl and serve immediately, or cover and refrigerate for up to 2 hours.

MAKES ABOUT 1½ CUPS

DIVINE DIPPERS JUDITH SUGGESTS SERVING THIS WITH SLICES OF DAIKON OR THOSE GORGEOUS ROUND RADISHES THAT ARE REDDISH INSIDE.

Toni Oberholzer's Tsatziki

When my friend Toni was pregnant with her first child, Wyatt, she used to go to a local diner and request a sandwich made with tsatziki, bacon, and tomato. It was unbelievably delicious and, although it wasn't on their menu, they always made it for her, albeit reluctantly. Later, when I wrote about it for the *Boston Phoenix*, a local newspaper, the owners added it to their menu, and I am told it's now one of their most popular items. Of course, this tsatziki is great as the dip it was intended to be, though it also makes a tasty garnish for burgers, omelets, or steak sandwiches.

2 cups Yogurt Cheese (page 16)
1 large European cucumber, quartered lengthwise and thinly sliced
2 garlic cloves, minced
$\frac{1}{4}$ cup finely chopped fresh mint leaves, plus more for garnish
$\frac{1}{4}$ to $\frac{1}{2}$ teaspoon kosher salt, to your taste

1. Place all the ingredients in a medium-size mixing bowl and combine well.

2. Transfer to a serving bowl and serve immediately, garnished with chopped mint, or cover and refrigerate for up to 2 days.

Variation: Substitute goat cheese for the yogurt cheese.

MAKES ABOUT 2$\frac{1}{4}$ CUPS

DIVINE DIPPERS WARMED PITA TRIANGLES OR CHERRY TOMATOES

Tropical Fruit Salsa

The truth is that there are enough salsa recipes for an entire other book, but I couldn't resist including this one, which is more unusual than most. Try it with grilled fish.

$\frac{1}{2}$ pineapple, peeled, cored, and finely chopped
1 ripe mango, peeled, pitted, and finely chopped
1 ripe papaya, peeled, seeded, and finely chopped
1 medium-size red onion, finely chopped
1 jalapeño chile, seeded and finely minced
Juice and grated zest of 1 well-washed lime
Kosher salt to taste

1. Place everything in a medium-size nonreactive mixing bowl and mix well.

2. Transfer to a serving bowl and serve immediately, or cover and refrigerate for up to 2 hours.

MAKES ABOUT 3 CUPS

 DIVINE DIPPERS TORTILLA OR POTATO CHIPS

Baba Ghanoush with Fresh Cilantro and Mint

There seem to be as many ways to spell this Middle Eastern roasted eggplant puree as there are ways to prepare it: baba ghanoush, baba ganouj, baba gannoujh. Most recipes include tahini (sesame seed paste), garlic, lemon juice, olive oil, and parsley. I have added lemon zest for greater intensity of flavor and substituted cilantro for the parsley, but otherwise it's fairly true to its roots. You can also try adding a few chopped fresh tomatoes.

1 large eggplant, pricked with the tines of a fork
1 to 2 garlic cloves, to your taste, minced
3 tablespoons tahini
2 tablespoons fresh lemon juice
2 teaspoons finely grated lemon zest
$1/4$ cup finely chopped scallions (white and green parts)
$1/4$ cup finely chopped fresh cilantro leaves, plus more for garnish
$1/4$ cup finely chopped fresh mint leaves
Kosher salt to taste
Cayenne pepper to taste (optional)
Pomegranate seeds for garnish (optional)
Toasted pistachios for garnish (optional)

1. Preheat the oven to 425°F.

2. To roast the eggplant, place it in the oven, turning occasionally, until it is very soft, about 45 minutes. Set aside to cool; when it is cool enough to handle, cut it in half, scoop out the flesh, and transfer it to a colander to drain. Press out and discard any liquid.

3. Place the eggplant flesh, garlic, and tahini in a food processor and pulse until combined. Transfer to a medium-size mixing bowl, add the lemon juice, zest, scallions, cilantro, and mint, season with salt and cayenne, if desired, and mix well. Cover and refrigerate at least 1 hour and up to overnight to let the flavors develop.

4. Transfer to a serving bowl and serve garnished with chopped cilantro and the pomegranate seeds and toasted pistachios, if desired.

MAKES ABOUT 2 CUPS

DIVINE DIPPERS WARMED PITA TRIANGLES, PITA CHIPS, OR THE CRUDITÉS OF YOUR CHOICE

Lauren's Famous Guacamole

Beginning at about age four, my daughter, Lauren, became the guacamole maker in our house. She basically followed my recipe but added a few of her own touches. In fact, when my friend Steve Steinberg turned 50, his wife, Nancy, requested that Lauren make the guacamole for his surprise party; she went through a whole case of avocados. It isn't surprising that she no longer enjoys making it.

Be sure to buy avocados well ahead of when you want them; you can rarely find them ripe in the supermarket. To hasten the ripening process, place the avocado in a paper bag with an apple or a banana; it's ready when you can push it in slightly. If it's already ripe enough, simply refrigerate it; it won't continue to ripen in the fridge.

This guacamole is also great in sandwiches and omelets and on burgers.

2 perfectly ripe Hass avocados, peeled, pitted, and coarsely chopped
$1/2$ small beefsteak tomato, coarsely chopped
2 scallions (white and green parts), chopped
$1/4$ to $1/3$ cup chopped fresh cilantro leaves, to your taste
Pinch of cayenne pepper
$1/4$ teaspoon kosher salt
$1/8$ teaspoon red pepper flakes
1 tablespoon fresh lime juice
$1/4$ to $1/2$ fresh jalapeño or canned chipotle chile in adobo sauce (optional), finely minced
5 sprigs fresh cilantro for garnish
2 very thin slices lime for garnish

1. Place everything except the cilantro sprigs and lime slices in a medium-size mixing bowl and toss gently to mix. Do not overmix; it should be somewhat chunky.

2. Transfer to a serving bowl and serve immediately, garnished with the cilantro sprigs and lime slices, or place a few avocado pits in the guacamole (to prevent discoloration), cover, and refrigerate for up to 8 hours.

MAKES ABOUT 1 $1/2$ CUPS

DIVINE DIPPERS TORTILLA OR PITA CHIPS, WARMED PITA TRIANGLES, OR ENDIVE SPEARS

Nancy Olin's Black Bean and Corn Salsa

Nancy describes this salsa as "really pretty and mind-blowingly good." Don't even think of making it with canned or frozen corn—it must be made in the summertime with the freshest corn off the cob you can find.

5 tablespoons olive oil
1 garlic clove, minced
2 teaspoons ground cumin
1 tablespoon chili powder
Pinch of cayenne pepper
4 ears fresh corn, kernels cut off the cob
3 tablespoons water
One 15.5-ounce can black beans, drained and rinsed
½ cup minced scallions (white and green parts), plus more for garnish
Juice of 1 lime
Salt and freshly ground black pepper to taste

1. Place a medium-size skillet over medium heat and, when it is hot, add 2 tablespoons of the olive oil, the garlic, cumin, chili powder, and cayenne and cook for 1 minute. Add the corn and water, cover, and cook until the corn is tender, about 3 minutes.

2. Off the heat, add the beans, scallions, lime juice, and remaining 3 tablespoons oil, season with salt and black pepper, and stir well to combine. Cover and refrigerate for at least 2 hours and up to overnight to let the flavors develop.

3. Transfer to a serving bowl and serve garnished with chopped scallions.

Variation: Add chopped red bell pepper, tomatoes, and/or fresh cilantro to your taste.

MAKES ABOUT 3½ CUPS

 DIVINE DIPPERS TORTILLA CHIPS

Mark's Classic Clam Dip

My husband, Mark, grew up eating this dip regularly and takes great pride in making it. According to Mark, "It's perfection in its simplicity. You can vary what you dip into it but you don't mess with the ingredients."

> One 8-ounce package cream cheese, at room temperature, or 1 cup
>   Yogurt Cheese (page 16)
> One 6.5-ounce can minced clams, drained, reserving the liquid
> ¼ cup minced red onion
> Tabasco sauce to taste

1. Place the cream cheese in a shallow bowl and mash. Add the clams and onion and mash again. Add 3 to 4 tablespoons of the reserved clam juice and mash until it has the consistency you like. Season with Tabasco.

2. Transfer to a serving bowl and serve immediately, or cover and refrigerate for up to 3 hours.

MAKES 1½ CUPS

DIVINE DIPPERS POTATO OR CORN CHIPS, BABY CARROTS OR CARROT STICKS, CELERY STICKS, OR ENDIVE SPEARS

David Tobias's Papa Harold's Chopped Chicken Liver Pâté

When I was a child, my mother served chopped chicken liver when she had dinner parties. I loved to sneak into the kitchen and eat huge amounts of it. So naturally when I was looking for a recipe, I called my mother, who confessed to me that the recipe wasn't hers. The dish was purchased from a store and called Mrs. Goldberg's Chopped Chicken Liver Pâté. Alas, I haven't been able to find Mrs. Goldberg or her chopped chicken liver pâté.

I got this recipe from David Tobias, who makes it for every Jewish holiday and serves it with roasted red peppers.

1 tablespoon olive oil
4 to 5 small onions (sweet or yellow), finely chopped
2 pounds chicken livers, trimmed and patted dry
6 large hard-boiled eggs, peeled
Sweet sherry to taste
Kosher salt and freshly ground black pepper to taste

1. Preheat the oven to 450°F. Lightly grease a baking sheet.
2. Place a large skillet over medium heat and, when it is hot, add the oil. Add the onions and cook, stirring, until golden, 10 to 12 minutes. Set aside.
3. Place the livers on the prepared baking sheet and bake for 5 minutes. Change the setting to broil and broil until slightly crispy. Remove from the oven and drain on paper towels.
4. Place the onions, livers, and eggs in a food processor and process until the mixture has a slightly chunky consistency. Season with the sherry, salt, and pepper.
5. Transfer to a serving bowl and serve immediately, or cover and refrigerate overnight.

MAKES 1 1/2 TO 2 CUPS

DIVINE DIPPERS SMALL SQUARES OF RYE BREAD

Andy Husbands's Hot Crabmeat Dip

When Andy gave me this dip recipe, it was 1996 and he had just opened his first Boston restaurant, Tremont 647. He's been very busy since then—he now owns Sister Sorel and Rouge, both in the same neighborhood.

This dip is best made on the day you are going to serve it; if you would like to do some work ahead of time, mix everything together and add the crabmeat just prior to cooking. This dip is also great uncooked.

1 teaspoon olive oil
2 garlic cloves, finely chopped
$\frac{1}{2}$ cup mayonnaise
1 celery stalk, finely diced
1 small shallot, finely diced
1 to 2 tablespoons fresh lemon juice, to your taste
1 tablespoon chopped fresh Italian parsley leaves
2 teaspoons peeled and grated fresh horseradish
2 teaspoons Dijon mustard
1 teaspoon fresh thyme leaves
$\frac{1}{2}$ teaspoon red pepper flakes
1 cup fresh crabmeat, picked over for shells and cartilage
Salt and freshly ground black pepper to taste

1. Preheat the oven to 450°F.

2. Place a small skillet over medium-high heat and, when it is hot, add the oil. Add the garlic and cook, stirring, until golden, about 2 minutes. Place the garlic in a medium-size mixing bowl, add the mayonnaise, celery, shallot, lemon juice, parsley, horseradish, mustard, thyme, and red pepper flakes, and mix well. Using a spatula, lightly fold in the crabmeat. Season with salt and pepper.

3. Transfer to a small casserole and bake until light brown, 10 to 15 minutes. Serve immediately.

MAKES ABOUT 2 CUPS

 DIVINE DIPPERS CRUDITÉS OF YOUR CHOICE, CROSTINI, OR CRACKERS

cheesy dips

4

- Todd English's Herbed Goat Cheese Spread
- Sarah Shaw's Goat Cheese and Sun-Dried Tomato Dip
- Spicy Feta Dip with Fresh Mint and Cilantro
- Truffled Goat Cheese Spread
- Horseradish Cheddar Dip
- Goat Cheese Spread with Dried Apricots and Pistachios
- Roasted Walnut and Gorgonzola Dip
- Chutney Cheddar Dip
- Hot Camembert Cheese with Cranberries and Sweet and Spicy Pecans
- Lizzy Shaw's Creamy Dreamy Gorgonzola Dip
- Roasted Red Pepper and Ricotta Dip
- Lizzy's Awesome Chunky Blue Cheese Dip with Herbs

Todd English's Herbed Goat Cheese Spread

I came across this great dip when I wrote *The Figs Table* with Todd English in 1998 (Simon & Schuster). Todd rarely used it as a dip but instead dolloped it on pizza, salads, pasta, and burgers and swirled it into polenta. It's not only versatile, it's also a snap to make and lasts up to a week.

1 cup crumbled goat cheese or ricotta cheese, at room temperature
1 teaspoon chopped fresh rosemary leaves
1 teaspoon chopped fresh sage leaves
1 teaspoon chopped fresh oregano leaves
Kosher salt to taste (depends on the saltiness of the goat cheese)
Pinch of freshly ground black pepper

1. Place the goat cheese in a medium-size mixing bowl and mash well. Add the remaining ingredients and mix until well combined.

2. Transfer to a serving bowl and serve immediately, or cover and refrigerate for up to 1 week. If refrigerated, let soften a bit before serving, if desired.

MAKES 1 CUP

DIVINE DIPPERS CELERY STICKS, BABY CARROTS OR CARROT STICKS, GRAPE OR CHERRY TOMATOES, ENDIVE SPEARS, BLANCHED ASPARAGUS, PITA CHIPS, OR FRENCH BREAD TOASTS

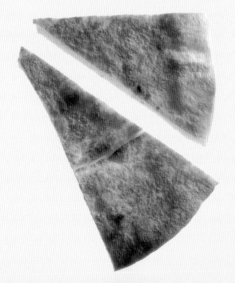

Sarah Shaw's Goat Cheese and Sun-Dried Tomato Dip

This is without a doubt the best use of sun-dried tomatoes I have ever had and a great example of the sum being more than its parts. When Sarah first told me about this dip, I was skeptical because I never really have loved sun-dried tomatoes. However, ever since she gave me the recipe, I have been making and remaking this dip, with total enjoyment. Try it as well as a filling for omelets or as a topping for burgers.

$\frac{1}{2}$ cup sun-dried tomatoes
$\frac{1}{2}$ cup boiling water
$\frac{1}{4}$ cup olive oil
1 to 2 garlic cloves, to your taste, minced
1 log goat cheese (10 to 12 ounces)
Kosher salt to taste
Finely chopped fresh basil leaves for garnish (optional)

1. Place the tomatoes in a small heatproof bowl and cover with the boiling water. Let stand until softened, 8 to 15 minutes, depending on the hardness of the tomatoes. Drain and return to the bowl. Add the olive oil and garlic, cover, and refrigerate for 2 to 3 days to let the flavors develop.

2. Add the goat cheese and mash with a fork. Season with salt. Transfer to a serving bowl and serve immediately, garnished with basil, if desired, or cover and refrigerate for up to 1 week. If refrigerated, let soften a bit before serving, if desired.

MAKES ABOUT 2 CUPS

DIVINE DIPPERS SARAH SAYS, "I LIKE TO SPREAD THIS ON THE FAT END OF ENDIVE LEAVES AND ARRANGE THEM AROUND A PLATE OF RADISHES. IT'S GOOD WITH CHILLED ASPARAGUS SPEARS, TOO." I LIKE IT ON TRIANGLES OF THINLY SLICED BLACK BREAD.

Spicy Feta Dip with Fresh Mint and Cilantro

Inspired by an appetizer I once had of feta cheese marinated in cumin, coriander, and red pepper flakes, this dip is herby, spicy, savory, and creamy. It's great on burgers, on eggs, or with anything accompanied by black olives.

8 ounces feta cheese, crumbled
$\frac{1}{2}$ cup lowfat plain yogurt
$\frac{1}{2}$ teaspoon ground cumin
$\frac{1}{2}$ teaspoon ground coriander
$\frac{1}{2}$ to $\frac{3}{4}$ teaspoon red pepper flakes, to your taste
1 teaspoon grated orange zest, plus more for garnish
1 tablespoon chopped fresh cilantro leaves
1 tablespoon chopped fresh mint leaves

1. Place the feta and yogurt in a small mixing bowl and mash together with a fork until combined but still slightly chunky. Add the remaining ingredients and mix well.

2. Transfer to a serving bowl and serve immediately garnished with orange zest, or cover and refrigerate for up to 2 days.

MAKES ABOUT 1 CUP

DIVINE DIPPERS PITTED BLACK OLIVES, SLICED BAGUETTE, OR WARMED PITA TRIANGLES

Truffled Goat Cheese Spread

The amazing taste and ease of preparation balance the expense of the ingredients in this dip. Truffle oil is produced when truffles are soaked in olive oil. The aroma and freshness weaken over time, so be sure to buy a fresh bottle and make this dip often. It's also fabulous spooned on top of mashed potatoes, sweet potatoes, or risotto or tossed with linguine.

> One 9-ounce log goat cheese, at room temperature
> 2 to 3 teaspoons truffle oil, or to your taste
> 4 radishes, trimmed and grated
> ¼ cup chopped fresh chives

1. Place all the ingredients in a small mixing bowl and mash together with a fork to combine.

2. Transfer to a serving bowl and serve immediately, or cover and refrigerate for up to 1 week. If refrigerated, let soften a bit before serving, if desired.

Variation: Substitute one 8-ounce package cream cheese for the goat cheese.

MAKES ABOUT 1½ CUPS

DIVINE DIPPERS CUCUMBER ROUNDS OR TRIANGLES OF THINLY SLICED PUMPERNICKEL BREAD

Horseradish Cheddar Dip

The first time I made this dip, I started out with a tablespoon of horseradish. It wasn't enough, but being a bit horseradish shy, I added only one more. Still it wasn't enough, and so, tasting after each addition of yet one more tablespoon, I eventually arrived at a whopping eight.

Horseradish has been used as an aphrodisiac, a rub for lower back pain, and a treatment for tuberculosis and rheumatism; it is also used as a bitter herb for Passover seders. About six million gallons of prepared horseradish are produced annually in the U.S.—enough to generously season sandwiches to reach 12 times around the world.

8 ounces sharp cheddar cheese, finely shredded (about 3 cups), at room
  temperature
$\frac{1}{4}$ cup sour cream or Yogurt Cheese (page 16)
2 tablespoons unsalted butter, at room temperature
$\frac{1}{2}$ cup prepared horseradish (without sugar)
1 tablespoon fresh lemon juice
Chopped fresh Italian parsley or cilantro leaves for garnish

1. Place the cheese, sour cream, and butter in a food processor and process until smooth. Add the horseradish and lemon juice and process until incorporated.

2. Transfer to a serving bowl and serve immediately, garnished with parsley, or cover and refrigerate for up to 2 weeks. If refrigerated, let soften before serving.

MAKES ABOUT 2 CUPS

 DIVINE DIPPERS CELERY STICKS, ZUCCHINI SPEARS, STEAMED TINY NEW POTATOES, TRIANGLES OF PUMPERNICKEL BREAD, OR FRENCH BREAD TOASTS

Goat Cheese Spread with Dried Apricots and Pistachios

A microplane grater is the only type of grater that will get the lemon zest fine enough for this creamy, salty, tangy, sweet spread.

¼ cup dried apricots, finely diced
¼ cup boiling water
1 log goat cheese (10 to 12 ounces), at room temperature
⅓ cup pistachio nuts, toasted (page 17) and finely chopped
¼ cup buttermilk
1 tablespoon finely chopped fresh mint leaves
1 to 2 teaspoons finely grated lemon zest, to your taste
Honey for drizzling (optional)

1. Place the apricots and boiling water in a small heatproof bowl and set aside until the water has been absorbed, about 15 minutes.

2. Add the goat cheese and mash well. Add the nuts, buttermilk, mint, and lemon zest and mash again.

3. Transfer to a serving bowl and serve immediately, drizzled with honey, if desired, or cover and refrigerate for up to 1 week. Let it come to room temperature before serving.

Variation: Substitute dried dates or figs for the apricots and pecans or walnuts for the pistachios.

MAKES ABOUT 2 CUPS

DIVINE DIPPERS TRIANGLES OF PUMPERNICKEL BREAD, CRACKERS, FRESH FIGS, OR STRAWBERRIES

Roasted Walnut and Gorgonzola Dip

Very rich and very creamy—in short, this is to die for.

4 ounces gorgonzola cheese, at room temperature
4 ounces (half of an 8-ounce package) cream cheese, at room temperature,
  or $1/2$ cup Yogurt Cheese (page 16)
$1/4$ cup cream (either light or heavy is fine)
1 teaspoon Cognac
4 tablespoons walnut halves, toasted (page 17)

1. Place the cheeses in a small mixing bowl and mash together with a fork. Gradually add the cream, 1 tablespoon at a time, and the Cognac and mash until well incorporated. Mix in 3 tablespoons of the walnuts.

2. Transfer to a serving bowl and serve immediately, garnished with the remaining 1 tablespoon walnuts, or cover and refrigerate for up to 3 days.

Variation: Substitute goat cheese for the cream cheese.

MAKES 1 TO 1$1/4$ CUPS

DIVINE DIPPERS ENDIVE SPEARS, RADISHES, OR TRIANGLES OF PUMPERNICKEL BREAD

Chutney Cheddar Dip

I first enjoyed this spicy and sweet dip in a ham sandwich piled with paper-thin apple slices and endive on black bread. I completely agree with Diana Vreeland, *Vogue* magazine's former editor-in-chief: "Chutney is marvelous. I'm mad about it. To me, it's very imperial."

Chutney is a piquant relish from India, usually made of fruit, spices, sugar, and vinegar. It can vary hugely in spiciness, so taste what's in your jar before adding it in.

> 8 ounces sharp cheddar cheese, finely shredded (about 3 cups), at room temperature
> 1/4 cup sour cream or Yogurt Cheese (page 16)
> 2 tablespoons unsalted butter, at room temperature
> 3 tablespoons chutney of your choice
> 1/2 teaspoon chili powder or cayenne pepper, or more to taste
> Finely chopped fresh Italian parsley or cilantro leaves for garnish

1. Place the cheese, sour cream, and butter in a food processor and process until smooth. Add the chutney and chili powder and process until the chutney is incorporated.

2. Transfer to a serving bowl and serve immediately, garnished with parsley, or cover and refrigerate for up to 2 weeks. If refrigerated, let it soften a bit before serving.

MAKES ABOUT 2 CUPS

DIVINE DIPPERS CRACKERS, APPLE SLICES, ENDIVE SPEARS, BABY CARROTS OR CARROT STICKS, OR CELERY STICKS

Hot Camembert Cheese with Cranberries and Sweet and Spicy Pecans

Hot, gooey, rich, creamy, sweet, and spicy all at the same time, this recipe is a winner. Be sure to buy a camembert round in a thin wood box; the box is necessary to the recipe.

One 8-ounce camembert round, frozen for at least 1 hour and up to 3 days
1 tablespoon brown sugar
1 heaping tablespoon chopped Sampson's Sweet and Spicy Pecans (see Note)
1 tablespoon dried cranberries

1. Preheat the oven to 300°F.

2. Carefully, using a sharp knife, scrap off the rind from the top of the camembert round. Return the round to the wood box. Spread the brown sugar over the surface, then top with the pecans and cranberries.

3. Place the box on a baking sheet, transfer it to the oven, and bake for 30 minutes.

4. As soon as you can handle it, remove the box and place the camembert on a serving plate. Serve immediately.

Note: Sampson's Sweet and Spicy Pecans are available on the Web at www.sampsonsnuts.com. If you can't get them quickly enough, substitute lightly roasted salted pecans.

Variation: Substitute 3 tablespoons chutney of your choice for the brown sugar, pecans, and cranberries, or brie for the camembert.

SERVES 6

 DIVINE DIPPERS TOAST ROUNDS, CRACKERS, BREAD STICKS, OR THE CRUDITÉS OF YOUR CHOICE

Lizzy Shaw's Creamy Dreamy Gorgonzola Dip

My childhood friend Lizzy Shaw only recently came to like blue cheese, but now she can't seem to get enough of it. This dip was inspired by one she got at a market in California; she's become such an aficionado that she was sure she could improve upon the one she bought. And she was right. This is also great on sandwiches, with Buffalo wings, and even on French fries!

Lizzy says to make sure not to get the waxy, hard kind of gorgonzola sold in wedges, which won't crumble and often doesn't have much flavor. You want the creamier version. If your gorgonzola stays in hard squares instead of crumbling, try mashing it a little with a fork. If it still won't soften up, or if the gorgonzola is too mild, add 2 tablespoons crumbled Rosenborg Danish blue cheese, which is available in many larger supermarkets, or another soft mild blue cheese, to make the dip creamier.

1 cup crumbled gorgonzola cheese
1 scallion (white and green parts), minced or thinly sliced
3½ heaping tablespoons sour cream or Yogurt Cheese (page 16)
1 heaping tablespoon cream cheese (regular, not whipped)
¼ teaspoon freshly ground black pepper
Pinch or ¼ teaspoon kosher salt, to your taste
1 teaspoon fresh lemon juice

1. Place all the ingredients in a small mixing bowl and mash with a fork until well combined.

2. Transfer to a serving bowl and set aside for 1 hour to let the flavors develop before serving, or cover and refrigerate overnight. If refrigerated, let it soften a bit before serving.

Variation: Make the whole thing with Rosenborg Danish blue cheese, or add a pinch of red pepper flakes for a little zing. Add about 1 tablespoon whole milk if you like a thinner dip. Thin it with about 2 tablespoons milk if you want to use it as a salad dressing, or just go ahead and add a big dollop of the spread "as is" to any salad and flip out at how good it is!

MAKES ABOUT 1¼ CUPS

 DIVINE DIPPERS LITTLE CRUNCHY CRACKERS, ENDIVE SPEARS, CELERY STICKS, OR BOILED TINY NEW POTATOES

Roasted Red Pepper and Ricotta Dip

This is perfect for those who want something low in fat but flavorful.

1 large bell pepper, roasted, peeled, and seeded (page 17), and cut into big chunks
1 to 2 garlic cloves, to your taste, sliced
1 scallion (white and green parts), ends trimmed
$^3/_4$ cup part-skim ricotta cheese
1 tablespoon cream cheese or Yogurt Cheese (page 16)
1 tablespoon chopped fresh mint leaves, plus more for garnish
1 tablespoon chopped fresh cilantro leaves
$^1/_4$ teaspoon freshly ground black pepper

1. Place the pepper in a food processor and pulse until chopped. Add the garlic and scallion and pulse until chopped. Add the remaining ingredients and process until well combined.

2. Transfer to a serving bowl and serve immediately, garnished with chopped mint, or cover and refrigerate for up to 4 hours.

MAKES ABOUT 1 CUP

DIVINE DIPPERS CELERY STICKS, BABY CARROTS OR CARROT STICKS, OR PITA OR BAGEL CHIPS

Lizzy's Awesome Chunky Blue Cheese Dip with Herbs

Here is another great blue cheese recipe from former blue cheese hater turned blue cheese fanatic Lizzy Shaw.

2 cups Danish blue cheese cut into ½-inch cubes
Good-quality olive oil to cover
1 teaspoon fresh rosemary leaves
1 teaspoon chopped fresh oregano leaves
1 teaspoon fresh thyme leaves
Pinch of freshly ground black pepper
Pinch of red pepper flakes
Kosher salt to taste

1. Place all the ingredients in a medium-size mixing bowl, toss together gently, cover, and refrigerate at least overnight and up to 5 days to let the flavors develop.

2. To serve, fish out the cheese chunks with a fork (they look pretty with the herb flakes), reserving the herbed oil, and place them in a bowl. To make more dip, continue to add more cheese to the marinating oil until it gets too cloudy and looks ugly.

MAKES 2 CUPS

DIVINE DIPPERS LIGHTLY STEAMED BROCCOLI FLORETS, FRENCH BREAD TOASTS, OR TRIANGLES OF PUMPERNICKEL BREAD

Measurement Equivalents

Please note that all conversions are approximate.

LIQUID CONVERSIONS

U.S.	METRIC
1 tsp	.5 ml
1 tbs	.15 ml
2 tbs	.30 ml
3 tbs	.45 ml
¼ cup	.60 ml
⅓ cup	.75 ml
⅓ cup + 1 tbs	.90 ml
⅓ cup + 2 tbs	.100 ml
½ cup	.120 ml
⅔ cup	.150 ml
¾ cup	.180 ml
¾ cup + 2 tbs	.200 ml
1 cup	.240 ml
1 cup + 2 tbs	.275 ml
1¼ cups	.300 ml
1⅓ cups	.325 ml
1½ cups	.350 ml
1⅔ cups	.375 ml
1¾ cups	.400 ml
1¾ cups + 2 tbs	.450 ml
2 cups (1 pint)	.475 ml
2½ cups	.600 ml
3 cups	.720 ml
4 cups (1 quart)	.945 ml
	(1,000 ml is 1 liter)

WEIGHT CONVERSIONS

U.S. / U.K.	METRIC
½ oz	14 g
1 oz	28 g
1½ oz	48 g
2 oz	57 g
2½ oz	66 g
3 oz	85 g
3½ oz	100 g
4 oz	113 g
5 oz	142 g
6 oz	170 g
7 oz	200 g
8 oz	227 g
9 oz	255 g
10 oz	284 g
11 oz	312 g
12 oz	340 g
13 oz	368 g
14 oz	400 g
15 oz	425 g
1 lb	454 g

OVEN TEMPERATURES

°F	GAS MARK	°C
250	½	120
275	1	140
300	2	150
325	3	165
350	4	180
375	5	190
400	6	200
425	7	220
450	8	230
475	9	240
500	10	260

Index

Note: Pages in *italics* refer to photographs.

about the author

Sally Sampson is a Boston-based food journalist whose work has appeared in *Bon Appétit*, *Food & Wine*, the *Boston Globe*, and other publications. She is the author of several cookbooks, including *Party Nuts!* and *The $50 Dinner Party*, and the co-author of several cookbooks.

acknowledgments

Thanks and thanks again to my testers, dippers, and contributors: Sydny Miner, Carla Glasser, Jenny Alperen, Nancy Olin and Steve Steinberg, Toni and Dan Oberholzer, Jenny DeBell and Bob Schlenig, Donna Levin and Russ Robinson, Lizzy Shaw, Cynthia Stewart, Susan and Gordon Benett, Rayna and Kevin Sampson, Judi Fitts, Stan Frankenthaler, Keri Fisher, Sandra Fairbank, Susan Orlean and John Gillespie, Peter and Annette Nirenberg, Sarah Shaw, Judith and Bob Shaw, Sharon Smith and James Mauch, David Zebny, Ginny George and Bob Carey, Chris Schlesinger, and Todd English.